BACK TO TITANIC

PARAMOUNT PICTURES AND TWENTIETH CENTURY FOX PRESENT A LIGHTSTORM ENTERTAINMENT PRODUCTION A JAMES CAMERON FILM "TITANIC" LEONARDO DiCAPRIO KATE WINSLET BILLY ZANE KATHY BATES FRANCES FISHER BERNARD HILL JONATHAN HYDE DANNY NUCCI GLORIA STUART DAVID WARNER AND BILL PAXTON MUSIC BY JAMES HORNER COSTUME DESIGNER DEBORAH L. SCOTT MUSIC SUPERVISOR RANDY GERSTON CO-PRODUCERS AL GIDDINGS GRANT HILL SHARON MANN FILM EDITORS CONRAD BUFF, A.C.E. JAMES CAMERON RICHARD A. HARRIS PRODUCTION DESIGNER PETER LAMONT DIRECTOR OF PHOTOGRAPHY RUSSELL CARPENTER, A.S.C. SPECIAL VISUAL EFFECTS BY DIGITAL DOMAIN EXECUTIVE PRODUCER RAE SANCHINI PRODUCED BY JAMES CAMERON AND JON LANDAU

  PG-13 PARENTS STRONGLY CAUTIONED Some Material May Be Inappropriate for Children Under 13

Soundtrack Available on SONY CLASSICAL   Read the book by HARPERPERENNIAL
Featuring "My Heart Will Go On" Performed by Celine Dion

WRITTEN AND DIRECTED BY JAMES CAMERON

titanicmovie.com

ISBN 0-634-00127-2

HAL•LEONARD®
CORPORATION
7777 W. BLUEMOUND RD. P.O. BOX 13819 MILWAUKEE, WI 53213

Visit Hal Leonard Online at
www.halleonard.com

AN IRISH PARTY IN THIRD CLASS

Traditional
Arranged by
GAELIC STORM

Moderately fast in 4

Play 3 times

JOHN RYAN'S POLKA

BLARNEY PILGRIM
Moderately fast

ALEXANDER'S RAGTIME BAND

Words and Music by
IRVING BERLIN
Arranged by
JOHN ALTMAN

THE PORTRAIT

By JAMES HORNER

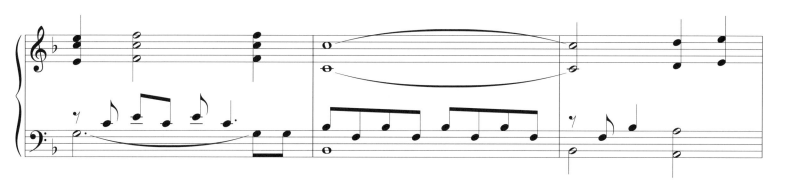

JACK DAWSON'S LUCK

By JAMES HORNER

THE HUMOURS OF CALEDON

19

THE RED-HAIRED LASS

Faster

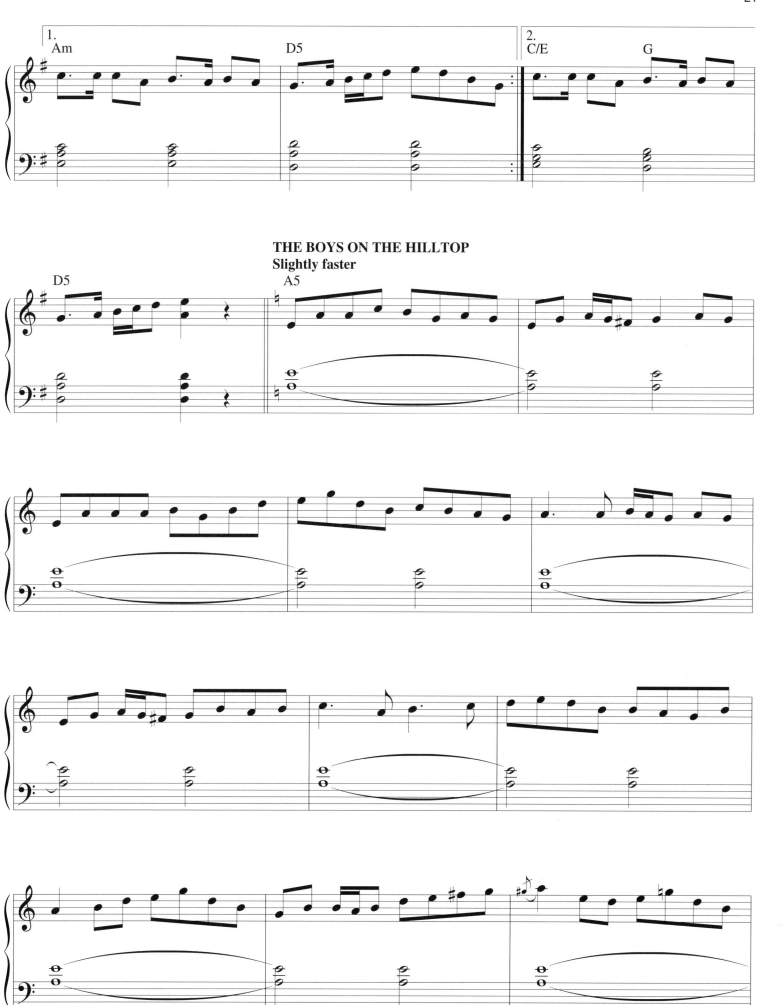

THE BOYS ON THE HILLTOP
Slightly faster

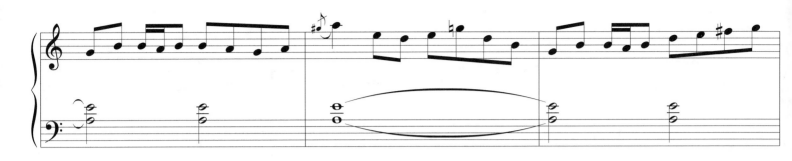

THE BUCKS OF ORANMORE

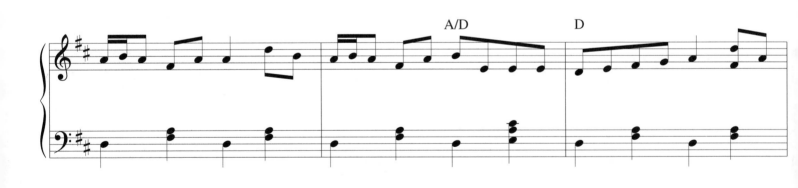

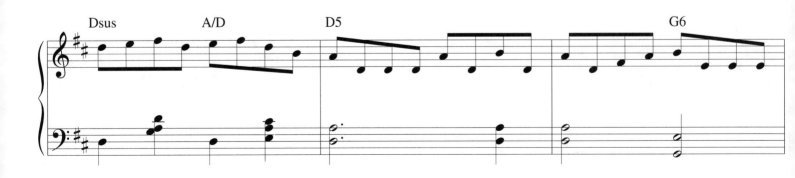

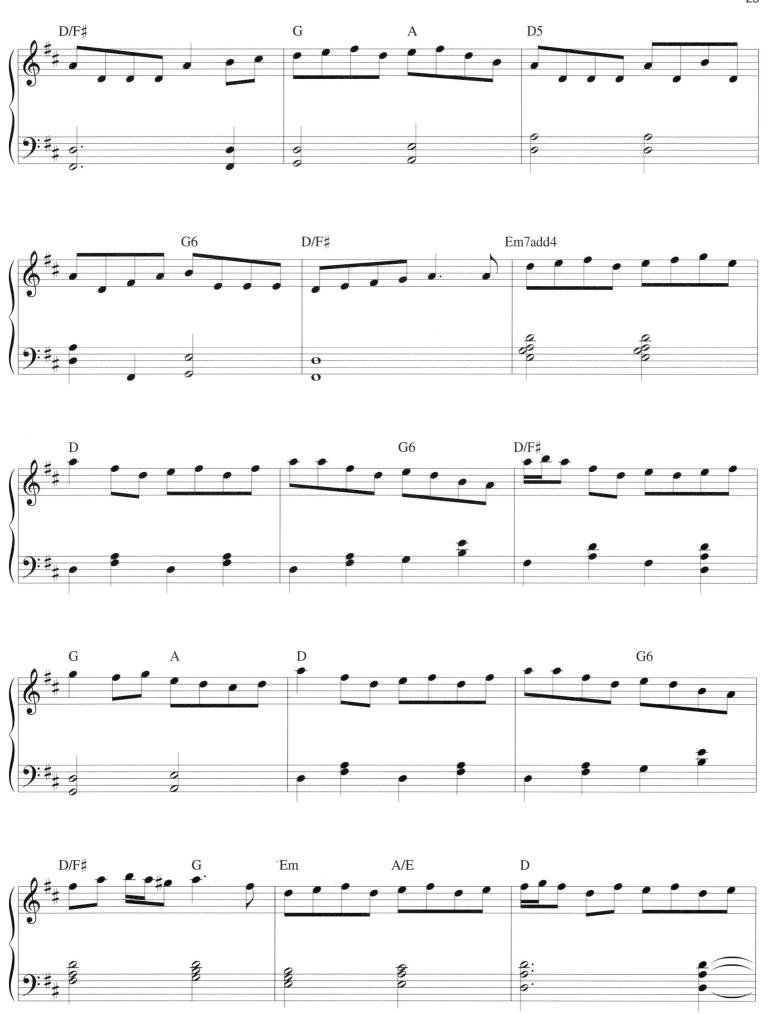

A BUILDING PANIC

By JAMES HORNER

Driving

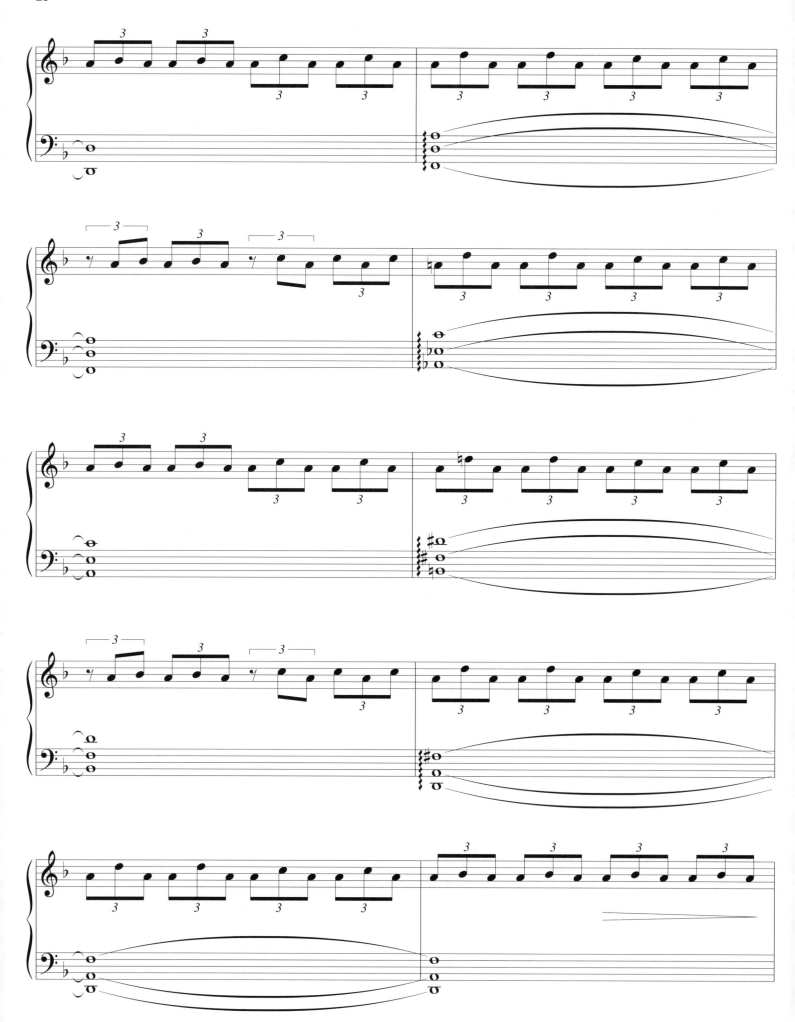

COME JOSEPHINE, IN MY FLYING MACHINE

Words by ALFRED BRYAN
Music by FRED FISCHER
Arranged by JOHN ALTMAN

NEARER MY GOD TO THEE

Text by SARAH ADAMS
Music by LOWELL MASON
Arranged by JONATHAN EVANS-JONES

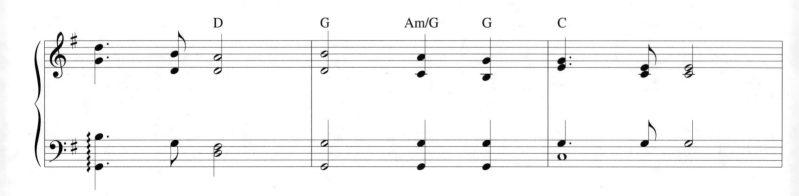

A SHORE NEVER REACHED

By JAMES HORNER

Moderately, expressively

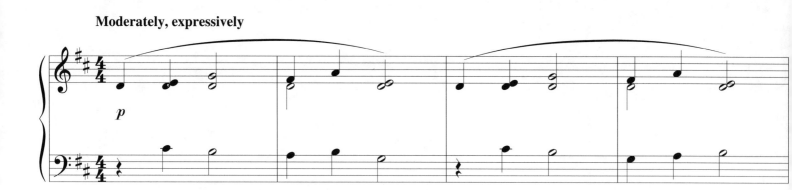

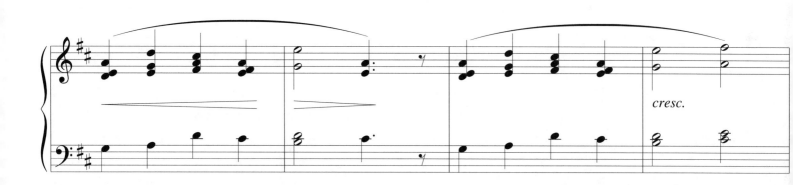

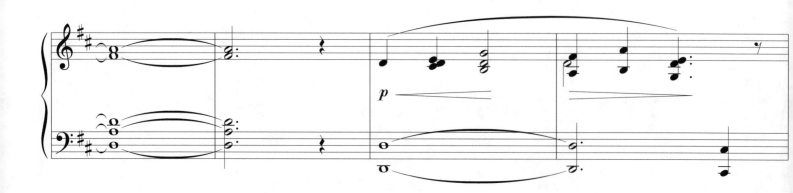

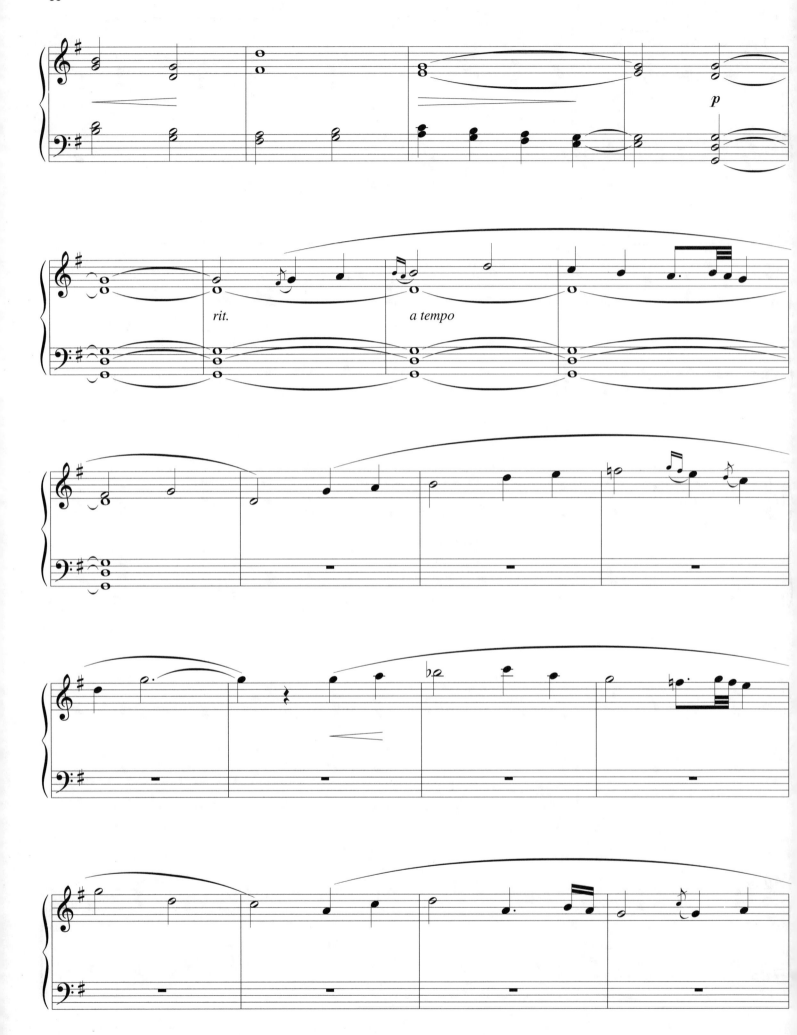

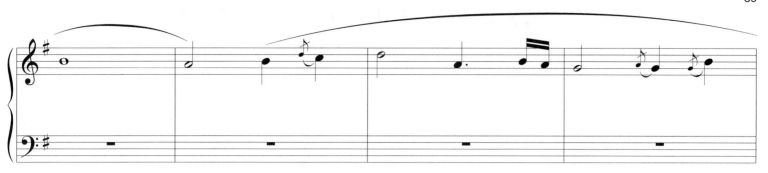

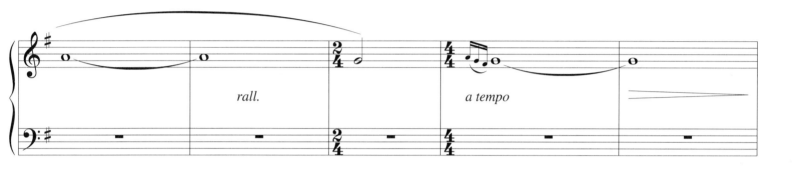

rall.

a tempo

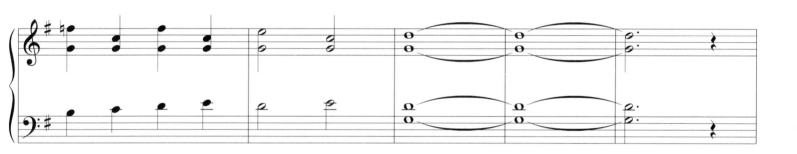

rit.

MY HEART WILL GO ON
(Love Theme from 'Titanic')

Music by JAMES HORNER
Lyric by WILL JENNINGS

EPILOGUE - THE DEEP AND TIMELESS SEA

By JAMES HORNER

Slowly, with expression